Soul Wounds

Dr.Kellie Diane

 **"On This Day:**

The Journey Begins"

Publisher Awareherness Press Publishers

Awareherness@gmail.com

LCCN 2024919097

ISBN: 9781965702000

Welcome to Your Journey of Healing, Self-Awareness, and Self-Love.

Dearest Soul,

You hold in your hands a transformative tool designed to guide you on a path of healing and self-discovery. This journal is more than just a collection of pages; it is a sacred space where you can explore the depths of your soul, confront your wounds, and nurture your spirit.

Life can leave us with invisible scars: those experiences and emotions that weigh heavily on our hearts. Acknowledging these soul wounds is the first step toward liberation. Through reflection, intention, and mindfulness, you can begin to mend the fragmented parts of yourself and cultivate a deeper sense of wholeness.

Each page invites you to engage with your thoughts and feelings, providing prompts and exercises that encourage introspection and growth. Remember, this journey is uniquely yours; there is no right or wrong way to heal. Allow yourself the grace to explore at your own pace, and trust that each step you take brings you closer to a more vibrant, authentic self.

As you embark on this journey, may you find clarity, strength, and the profound peace that comes from understanding and loving yourself fully.

With compassion and encouragement,

Dr Kellie Diane

Abandonment

1. What experience did you have that created your wound of abandonment?

1. How did this wound affect you throughout your adulthood?

Injustice

1. What experience did you have that created your wound of injustice?

1. How did this wound affect you throughout your adulthood?

Betrayal

1. What experience did you have that created your wound of betrayal?

1. How did this wound affect you throughout your adulthood?

Rejection

1. What experience did you have that created your wound of rejection?

1. How did this wound affect you throughout your adulthood?

Humiliation

1. What experience did you have that created your wound of humiliation?

1. How did this wound affect you throughout your childhood?

The Awakening

1. Have you experienced an awakening moment? If so describe it.

2. What old way of thinking do you need to shed that no longer serves a purpose in your life?

....

....

....

....

....

....

....

....

....

....

....

....

....

....

....

....

....

....

....

....

....

....

Acknowledging your wounds

1. What day did you start your healing journey? Describe your feelings on that day.

2. What prompted you to initiate this journey?

3. What are your fears concerning this journey?

Damage of unhealed wounds

1. What behavior have you displayed that was damaging to yourself?

2. Describe each behavior and it's impact on your life

3. What event in your past was a repetitive cycle that was taught to you as a child?

4. Do you know who you are? Write a description below without all of your achievements and or/title.

The journey to healing

1. What emotions did you encounter? How did you respond?

2. What words of affirmation have you incorporated in your life?

....
....
....
....
....
....
....
....
....
....
....
....
....
....
....
....
....
....
....
....
....
....
....

3. What questions about your childhood wounds do you wish you could ask your parents?

Living in wellness

1. What purpose have you discovered about yourself?

2. Are there people that you need to reposition in your life? Describe your plan for repositioning each person.

3. What techniques have you found effective in raising your awareness?

Your eyes through the brand new you

1. Now that you have taken the journey, have you discovered your purpose? Describe it below

----

2. Describe something new that you have discovered about yourself on this journey.

....
....
....
....
....
....
....
....
....
....
....
....
....
....
....
....
....
....
....
....
....
....

3. Do you believe that telling your story(your truth) could be significant to the world?

....
....
....
....
....
....
....
....
....
....
....
....
....
....
....
....
....
....
....
....
....
....
....

Self-Reflection Questions

1. What do you believe are the limiting beliefs that hold you back from reaching your full potential?

----

2. How do you define success, and how does that definition influence your actions and decisions?

....
....
....
....
....
....
....
....
....
....
....
....
....
....
....
....
....
....
....
....
....
....
....

3. What are your top strengths, and how can you leverage them to achieve your goals?

----

4. In what areas of your life do you feel most fulfilled, and what factors contribute to that sense of fulfillment?

5. What negative thought patterns or behaviors do you want to release in order to create space for positive change?

6. How do you typically respond to challenges or setbacks, and what strategies can you use to cultivate resilience?

7. What are your core values, and how do they guide your choices and priorities?

8. How do you nurture your physical, mental, and emotional well-being on a daily basis?

....
....
....
....
....
....
....
....
....
....
....
....
....
....
....
....
....
....
....
....
....
....
....

9. What dreams or aspirations have you put on hold, and what steps can you take to reignite your passion for them?

10. How can you practice more self-compassion and kindness towards yourself in moments of difficulty or self-doubt?

Exercises

11. Create a vision board that represents your goals, dreams and aspirations for the future. Describe why you chose each goal.

....

....

....

....

....

....

....

....

....

....

....

....

....

....

....

....

....

....

....

....

....

....

12. Write a letter to your future self outlining the person you aspire to become and the goals you aim to achieve.

13. Practice gratitude journaling by listing three things you are grateful for each day.

....

....

....

....

....

....

....

....

....

....

....

....

....

....

....

....

....

....

....

....

....

....

14. Engage in a mindful meditation exercise for ten days to reduce stress and cultivate present-moment awareness. Write down the daily exercises and explain your rationale for choosing each exercise. Also, record their effectiveness.

15. It's important to take the time to conduct a values assessment to identify your core values and ensure that your actions align with them. "What are 10 positive values that you appreciate about yourself?" "How can you better align yourself with them?"

----

16. Develop a self-care plan that includes activities and practices that nourish your mind, body, and spirit.

....
....
....
....
....
....
....
....
....
....
....
....
....
....
....
....
....
....
....
....
....
....
....
....

17. Experiment with positive affirmations by writing down empowering statements that challenge negative self-talk.

18. Create a timeline of significant life events and reflect on how they have shaped your beliefs and behaviors.

19. Visualizing success can be a powerful tool. Consider practicing visualization techniques to imagine yourself achieving your goals or conquering challenges. What were the five techniques that you chose? How were they effective in your daily routine?

----

20. Identify a small action that you performed daily for 14 days to get closer to your goals/aspirations. Assess any changes, improvements, or insights gained over the 14-day period to determine their impact.

Prompts

21. Descibe a time when you felt most confident and empowered. What factors contributed to that sense of empowerment?

22. How do you define self-care, and what practices help you feel rejuvenated and balanced?

....
....
....
....
....
....
....
....
....
....
....
....
....
....
....
....
....
....
....
....
....
....
....

23. Identify one small action you can take today to move closer to a goal or aspiration you have set for yourself.

----

24. Imagine yourself five years from now. What accomplishments do you hope to celebrate by then?

25. What does it mean to live authentically for you, and how can you align your actions with your authentic self?

----

26. What does it mean to live authentically for you, and how can you align your actions with your authentic self?

27. Consider a fear or limiting belief that holds you back. What steps can you take to challenge and overcome it?

----

28. Reflect on a moment of failure or disappointment. What did you learn from that experience, and how did it shape your growth?

29. Identify one area of your life where you would like to invite more abundance or positivity. What actions can you take to manifest that change?

30. Write a letter of forgiveness to yourself or someone else, releasing any resentment or hurt that may be weighing you down.

----

31. Now that you've embarked on this journey and reached its conclusion, do you feel there are any wounds or aspects of your experience that require deeper attention or healing? Understanding that it can be difficult to navigate the healing process. Please take a moment to list the wounds below and share the techniques you plan to incorporate to assist in the healing process.

NOTES

Dearest Soul,

Congratulations on reaching the end of this journey. You have taken courageous steps toward healing, self-discovery, and transformation by engaging with these pages. Remember, this is not merely an ending but a beautiful beginning—an opportunity to integrate the insights and lessons you've uncovered into your daily life.

Embrace the growth you've experienced and carry it with you as you navigate the world. Know that healing is an ongoing process, and it's okay to revisit these reflections whenever you need guidance or encouragement. You are stronger and wiser than you may realize, and your journey continues to unfold in wondrous ways.

May you walk forward with an open heart, trusting in your ability to create a life filled with love, joy, and purpose. The light within you is a powerful force—share it with the world, and let it guide you toward your dreams.

With love and encouragement,

Dr Kellie Diane

www.ingramcontent.com/pod-product-compliance
Lightning Source LLC
Chambersburg PA
CBHW071007120626
46546CB00003B/974